NO LIMIT HOLD 'EM: THE BOOK OF BLUNDERS

15 COSTLY MISTAKES TO AVOID WHILE PLAYING NO LIMIT TEXAS HOLD 'EM

N. R. VILLARREAL

Outskirts Press, Inc.
Denver, Colorado

No Limit Hold 'EM:The Book of Blunders
15 Costly Mistakes To Avoid While Playing No Limit Texas Hold 'Em

Outskirts Press
http://www.outskirtspress.com

ISBN-10: 1-59800-723-8
ISBN-13: 978-1-59800-723-7

Printed in the United States of America

CONTENTS

SECTION ONE: GAME PLAY MISTAKES

SECTION TWO: MENTAL MISTAKES

INTRODUCTION

First, the good news; **poker is a game that can be beat**! It is a game where your skill and decision making ability matters. There is no doubt that luck plays a role in all poker sessions, but the most successful players find ways to minimize luck as much as possible. They are able to do this by making better decisions than their opponents and taking advantage of all their opponents' mistakes. The more mistakes their opponents make, the better the odds that they will walk away from the table with a nice profit.

Now the bad news**; it is impossible to play poker and not make any mistakes**. If you play long enough, you are going to make more than a few costly decisions. Even top pros, after sessions where they made hundreds of thousands of dollars in pure profit, will lament the two or three hands that they feel they should have played different. Instead of just being satisfied with a winning session, the top professional is going to be reviewing the hands that they didn't win and trying to determine if there was a way they could have played the hand differently. **The key is to make fewer mistakes than your opponents!**

Here is the best news; **this book will make you a better poker player**! With each chapter, your No-Limit Texas Hold 'Em skills will improve in both cash and tournament play! Once you are able to avoid the mistakes shown in this book, you will start making money in a more consistent manner than ever before! No Limit Hold 'Em allows the best player to fully maximize their profits by taking advantage of the weaker player's mistakes and poor decisions. The ways a poor player can make mistakes are countless. **This book will show you the most common mistakes being made and how you can take advantage of them!**

This book assumes that you have basic knowledge of No Limit Hold 'Em. The player that will benefit most from this book knows how to play NLH but wants to improve and win more consistently. If you are new to the game, you will want to visit one of the many web sites that offer explanation of the rules and game play for No Limit Texas Hold 'Em before reading through this book.

BASIC MATH IN POKER

You must understand the importance of math in poker before you can take your game to the next level. You only need a few basic math skills, the same skills you learn in elementary school, to grasp these concepts. Many of you are already familiar with every mathematical problem depicted in this book.

OUTS: Any cards that, as far as you know, are still in the deck and will help your hand become the winning hand. For example, if you hold the J-T and the board reads K-Q-2, what cards will make you a straight? Any Ace or Nine gives you a straight and there are four Aces and four Nines in the deck. That means that you have eight outs to make a straight. **Unless you know that one of your opponents has and Ace or Nine in their hand, you can count all eight cards are being available OUTS**.

<u>THE RULE OF 4 AND 2:</u> This is a very basic rule that you can use to estimate what your odds are of improving your hand by the river. First you must know how many OUTS you have.

Using the example above, you have 8 OUTS on the flop to make the nut straight. **If you have eight outs on the FLOP and want to know the probability of hitting one of those outs by the river, multiply the number of outs by four.** 8 x 4 = 32. We look at this number as a percentage. **You will hit one of your outs approximately 32% of the time if you see both the turn and river cards.**

With only one card to come, you multiply the outs by 2 to estimate your probability. On the **TURN**, if you still have eight outs to make a hand that you feel will be good enough to win the pot, you would multiply 8 by the number 2. 8 x 2 = 16. **You have about a 16% chance of hitting one of your outs with only one card to come.**

The Rule of 4 and 2 is not perfect, it is only an estimate. It should still give you a good idea of your odds.

<u>POT ODDS</u>: These are the odds that the pot is offering you to call a bet. If there is $20 in the pot and it costs you $10 to call, the pot is offering you 20 to 10, or 2 to 1 odds on your money.

<u>IMPLIED ODDS</u>: This is very important in NLH because the implied odds can be huge. Implied odds are the money that you can expect to win on future betting rounds, over and above what is in the pot right now. Here is an example of implied odds:

You have J-9. Your opponent has K-K. The flop is K-T-7. You will make a straight with either Queen or Eight. It costs you $20 to call and see the turn. The pot has $40. Your pot odds are 2 to 1 but your implied odds are even greater because if you are able to make your straight on the turn, you can see that your opponent will have little hesitation putting a lot of money into the pot with top set of Kings.

SECTION ONE
GAME PLAY MISTAKES

This section shows two players at completely different stages in their poker careers. FISH is a beginner and he will make all the mistakes amateur players make. HERO will then show the reader the correct action and thought process of a winning player.

THE EXAMPLES SHOWN ARE ALL ACTUAL HANDS, WITNESSED BY THE AUTHOR, THAT HAVE TAKEN PLACE AT VARIOUS CASINOS ACROSS THE COUNTRY. THE NAMES HAVE BEEN CHANGED BUT THE ACTION IS ALL TOO REAL.

CHAPTER ONE
GIVING ODDS

The name of the game is NO-LIMIT. Because you can bet any amount, a skilled player can manipulate the pot odds and protect his made hand against weaker drawing hands. In many situations, when a player fails to bet enough to discourage other players to call, they are making a huge mistake. They are giving their opponents, who have a worse hand than them at the moment, the correct price to call and try to outdraw them on a later street. We have all heard players cry and scream about taking a bad beat, but many times that "bad beat" occurred because the player failed to bet enough to protect his hand and win the pot on an earlier betting round

The game in all these examples will be the same:
9 handed cash game with $2/$5 blinds. Average stack size is $400.

Mistake #1: NOT PROTECTING A BIG PAIR PRE-FLOP

THE HANDS: Fish has pocket aces.

PRE-FLOP ACTION: Alvin, Dave and Lenny all limp in front of Fish, who is on the button. Fish raises to $15.

ANALYSIS: This is a very poor raise with a big hand. This bet is often referred to as a "pot sweetener" because it makes the pot a little bit bigger but it won't get any player that was going to stay in the hand to fold. **The last thing you want to do with a big pair is "sweeten" the pot and invite more players to see the flop.**

Currently, there are five players still active in this hand (both blinds that have not acted yet, Alvin, Dave and Lenny). The worst thing that could happen for Fish is to have one of the blinds call the $15. If this happens *(and there is no real reason to think that they won't call given the smallish raise and the potential to take down a big pot)* then the pot odds become that much better for each player in turn.

Even if both blinds fold, then Alvin is now looking at a pot size of $37 ($7 in blinds + three limpers at $5 per person for $15 + $15 from Larry). He has great pot odds of 3.7 to 1, but more importantly, it only costs him $10 to see the flop. This is a very inviting raise...the type of raise you can expect to encounter when playing LIMIT Hold 'Em. It costs two more bets to call to see this flop and more than likely this amount is too small to pass up. Remember, he voluntarily put money in the pot to see the flop...you will need a sizeable raise to keep him from seeing that flop. Since this is not LIMIT Hold 'Em, you need to take advantage of the structure and bet a much larger, less inviting amount if you do not want all of the players to call.

The only thing that Alvin has to worry about is if one Dave or Lenny put in a big raise...but that seems unlikely considering that they already had an opportunity to stick in a raise when it was their turn the first time around and they just limped. *(If one of the limpers did in fact raise, it would absolutely fantastic for Fish because he will have an opportunity to correct his previous mistake and either isolate an opponent with a big re-raise or take the pot down pre-flop by pushing all in.)*

This is very common pre-flop action and in most cases all three players that limped as well as one of the blinds will see the flop and try to outrun Fish's Aces.

Some of you may be wondering why it is a mistake to want more opponents in the pot when you not only have position, but you also have the best pre-flop hand possible. **A simple truth of Hold 'Em is that you want to isolate your opponents when you have big pairs or big cards. Big pairs like aces and kings lose most of their value when they are up against more than one or two opponents.** It is commonly said that it is better to win a small pot than lose a big one. Pocket aces are often very difficult to fold, so the best way to ensure a good win rate with them is by going up against as few opponents as possible. The only way to do this is by putting in a good size bet or raise.

*****

As a side note, if you only raise big when you have a big pair, you are also making a mistake. If your opponents know that you would only make a large raise pre-flop if you hold A-A or K-K, then you are giving them too much information and they might call with worse hands knowing that if they connect with a good flop they will take a big pot because you will have a hard time folding your big pair. You also need to be able to change gears from time to time and throw in a few big pre-flop raises with suited connectors or medium pairs if for nothing else than to better disguise your hands and make it harder for your opponents to put you on a hand. Just don't overdue it.

*****

WHAT WOULD HERO HAVE DONE?

The pot was already $22 when it was Fish's turn to act. **With a big pocket pair and no serious action in front of him, HERO would never make a bet less than the size of the pot.** HERO would have put in a bet of about $35. Could he bet more? Yes, but big pairs don't come around often and you would like to win some money with them. If you raise too much, everyone will fold. Just remind yourself that the more players that call your pre-flop raise, the more often you will lose because there are more possible hands in play.

One interesting point about this hand is Fish's position on the button. Many players know that the button player, because he gets to act last during the entire hand, will bluff more from this position than any other. All three limpers know that Fish might be trying to pick up the pot right now with a big bet because they all showed weakness by limping. His big raise from this position might not look like the big pair that it is.

If this was a tournament instead of a cash game, where survival is almost as important as collecting chips, a larger raise might be advised. You are most concerned with the first player, Alvin calling. If you don't raise enough, Alvin will call knowing that his call will probably entice others to call given the increasingly favorable pot odds. It is almost always correct to charge a larger price in tournaments than in cash games because once your chips are gone in a tournament, so are you. Hopefully you bet enough so that even if he calls, we will still be able to maintain our goal of only going up against one or at most two opponents.

Mistake #2: GIVING DRAWING HANDS GREAT ODDS TO CALL ON THE FLOP

THE HANDS: Joe has 5-5. Mike has 7-8s of diamonds. Brad has K-Q. **Fish has J-T.**

PRE-FLOP ACTION: Joe made it $20 to go pre-flop in early position. Mike, Brad and Fish all called. Both blinds folded. Pot is now $87.

THE FLOP: 4-9-T with one diamond. Fish is now in the lead with a pair of Tens.

Joe, Mike and Brad all check. Fish bets $20.

ANALYSIS: This is a terrible bet. That being said, this type of betting pattern is all too common with bad players. Look at all of the potential cards that will cause Fish to lose this hand: any 5, 6, J, Q, K. Since the Jack gives Fish top two pair, he will probably lose a bundle with that terrible turn card.

When it gets to Joe, there is a chance he will call this bet and take one off. He is hoping that he hits his 5 on the turn to make a set or that Fish is bluffing and his pair of 5s is good. He has reason to think that his pair might be good because why would Fish bet so small with a made hand? When a small bet like this is made, some players become suspicious of a trap being set, but even if Fish had a set of Tens he should have bet more than $20 because there are still so many ways he can be beat.

Mike will definitely call when it is his turn. He has an open ended straight draw with a possible backdoor flush draw. The backdoor flush draw is over a 20-1 shot to hit, but that added 5% possibility always helps. **Using the Rule of 4 & 2, Mike can calculate his probability of making his hand and see that he will make his straight better than 30% of the time.**

Even if Joe folds, the pot will contain $107 and since it only costs $20 to call, he is getting better than over 5-1 pot odds. Mike calls.

Brad had a gut-shot straight draw and two over-cards that could be good if they hit. **It has been said that you shouldn't draw to a gut-shot straight draw, but if the price is right you should make the call as long as you will have the nuts if you make your straight. You want to avoid taking a draw to less than the nuts in NLH because even if you get there, you could go broke!** If he counts his over-cards as outs (*and your opponents usually do*), he is looking at 10 outs. With the pot now offering $127, he is getting more than enough odds to see the next card.

Another problem with such a small bet is that any player drawing probably feels there is a decent chance that by calling this bet on the flop, the turn may be checked around or another small bet would be made…either way giving drawing players the knowledge that they will probably be able to see both the turn and river for very little money.

You should always be very aware of your table image. If you are consistently making bets that are too small on the flop and turn, many players will call raises out of position with drawing hands pre-flop, knowing that you will allow them the opportunity to draw out against you for a small price. You want your opponents to fear playing against you…not hoping that you are in the hand because you bet so small.

Where does that leave Fish? The pot is now $147 and he still has at least two remaining opponents. Even if he correctly determines that his hand is best right now, his big mistake of not betting enough has given his opponents the correct odds to out draw him and take down a good sized pot.

Ask yourself two questions:

A) How much should Fish bet if the Deuce of hearts falls on the turn and his opponents check to him?

B) What happens if an Ace of hearts falls on the turn and his opponents check to him?

For question A, this is one of the best cards that could fall for Fish. If none of his opponents raised his weak $20 bet on the flop, he must feel very confident that his hand is good right now. He needs to redeem himself and take this pot down right now! Nothing less than a pot sized bet is recommended. If he bets $150, it will very difficult for either Mike or Brad to call. They might shake their head and wonder how the Two of hearts could have helped Fish, but since they are only on draws themselves, this bet takes advantage of NLH and manipulates the pot odds so that they would be making a mistake to call the bet. Their pot odds are now about 2 to 1 ($150 to call a bet with a pot of $297) and there is only one card to come. **Because implied odds exist, the players might not need a full fifteen outs to call the bet, but the odds are still not in their favor. Still you must realize the psychological advantage of playing a hand where you bet $20 pre-flop, called $20 on the flop and now all of a sudden, someone drops a big $150 bet down and you are only on a draw!** Fish got very lucky with that turn card, but at least if he makes the right decision now, he can still win a good pot.

For question B, I hope that Fish was watching his opponents when that turn card was dealt. Did anyone give a reaction (either positive or negative)? **You should always be watching your opponents instead of the cards that are being turned over...the cards will still be there later for you to look at but you only get one chance to see that emotional reaction that some of your opponents give you.** Unless Fish got a reaction one way or another, and if they all check to him, you can see the pickle that he is in. Still, since they are all showing weakness and the pot is now a nice size, Fish has to try to take this down right now. There is just too good of a chance that his opponents are on draws. Not only that, if his opponents do not have the Ace and Fish makes a good sized bet, they will more than likely give him credit for the ace. **Many pros look at the ace as a great bluff card because an opponent that does not have an ace in his hand will often give credit for you having an ace in your hand more than any other in the entire deck.** How much should Fish bet? I am sure he is worried that one of his opponents stayed in there with a big Ace (*he did only bet $20 on the flop so it is reasonable to assume this*) or they might have had second or bottom pair with an Ace kicker on the flop and now they have two pair. Still he should fire out at least $100 with confidence. His opponents will not have the odds they need to draw and, unless they have an Ace in their hand, they will probably fold. Anything less would be too tempting to the players with draws to stay in and try to take down a very nice sized pot.

Why should Fish bet less for question B than question A? First of all, it is much more likely that his hand is ahead in question A than questions B so it makes sense that he put more of his money to go into that pot. Also, if the Ace did not hit any of your opponents, it may have reduced the number of outs that they were counting to beat you. After you bet $100 on the Ace falling, Brad is no longer counting on winning with his King or Queen so he might only think he has 4 outs left in the deck (in his mind he would count all four Jacks as outs). In this case he definitely does not have the odds he needs to call the turn bet.

WHAT WOULD HERO HAVE DONE ON THE FLOP?

The pot was $87. HERO flopped top pair weak kicker with position on his opponents. There was no real action pre-flop, a small open raise and three callers. All of his opponents checked to him on the flop. HERO knows that he holds a very vulnerable hand…not the type of hand with which you should try to milk money out of your opponents. HERO would bet about $60-$70 to take this pot down right now. The best thing going for him is that he has position in the hand, which is a huge advantage when you have a semi-weak holding.

Joe would definitely fold his meager pair of 5s.

If both players had enough money in play (in this example both players started the hand with $500), Mike might want to call the bet on the flop if he felt that he could break HERO if he made his straight on the turn. Still he would be forced to put in a lot of money on a draw and from the looks of HERO's flop bet, if Mike does not make his straight on the turn, HERO will very likely put in another big bet that Mike does not want to call. **Counting all 8 outs, Mike has a one in six chance of making his straight on the turn and he is only getting two to one odds to call the bet**. If he did decide the call the bet, he would be making a mathematical mistake.

Because of the size of the bet, Brad will probably not be counting his over-cards as outs. It looks like HERO could possibly have flopped two pair or a set meaning that the only card that Brad would count would be a Jack. **He has about an 8% chance to make this straight on the next card so there is no reasonable way he can call this bet.**
With a strong pot sized bet, HERO more than likely will take down the pot.

Mistake #3: MULTIPLE MISTAKES ON THE FLOP

THE HANDS: Matt has Q-T. Nick has J-T. Mark has A-K. **Fish has 7-7.**

PRE-FLOP ACTION: Matt made it $15 to go. Nick, Mark and Fish all called.

THE FLOP: K-Q-7.

Matt leads out for $20. Nick calls the $20. Mark raises to $60. Fish calls $60. Matt calls $40 more when it is his turn. Nick calls $40 and this round of betting is done.
Did you see all the mistakes made betting this flop? Think for a moment and see how many you can find.

Let's break down each player's actions on the flop:

MATT: There is definitely a problem with playing Q-T off-suit in early position in NLH. Unless you hit the flop just perfectly, you will more than likely lose money with this hand. Looking at the flop, Matt's bet of $20 is too small to get a lot of information and not enough to get rid of any drawing hands. He really has to hope that none of his opponents have any kind of hand or else they will call such a small bet. **Generally speaking, if you want to be a top player and respected opponent, if you are going to be the flop, you must bet at least half the pot. Otherwise your opponents are going to love playing pots with you because they will know you will let them "catch up" cheaply.** Since you are reading this book for advice, the best advice is not to play Q-T from early position and you won't find yourself in this situation. He compounds his error by calling the raise out of position hoping to pair his Ten or hit another Queen. The reason this play doesn't work is the number of opponents in the hand. The size of the raise was small so he can assume that all of the other players will call as well. There is no way he should think he has the best hand right now and there are so many possible hands in play that hitting one of his "outs" might only cost him more money by also making someone else a better hand. And he is playing out of position the rest of the way. He made a mistake with the weak lead of $20, and now he should fold and save his money for a better situation.

MARK: The pot was now $107. One opponent had made a weak lead at the pot and another opponent just called the weak lead. Mark is correct to raise, but he needs to stick in a raise to at least the size of the pot. If both Matt and Nick checked to him, he could have bet less than the pot, but now he has to assume that they too hit that flop and have at least marginal draws. He should be able to see that it is very likely that one of his opponents has J-T. There is a very good chance that his hand is the best right now so he should stick in a big enough raise to discourage anyone from drawing out on him. The beauty of NLH is the ability to manipulate the pot and he should do so right here. HERO would call the $20 bet and raise $100 more.

FISH: One of two things is happening here. Either he has decided to put in a trap and make his move of the turn or he doesn't understand the strength of a set. A set is a very powerful hand in NLH because it is disguised so well. I don't mind him setting a trap…but it seems too risky here because he will be up against too many opponents. **A trap works best if you are only against one opponent or if you have the absolute nuts.** FISH has neither and he should see that Mark's small raise will be called by at least one of the two remaining players. If Mark had put in a bigger raise, Mark's trap would have worked better.

After Mark's raise to $60, the pot is now $167. HERO would have come over the top of Mark for $200 (a raise of $140), and he would surely get any draws to fold. While his raise would probably force Mark to fold as well, it is still better to take this pot down now than to let 3 players try and draw out against you.

NICK: He has done nothing wrong at any time in the hand. The betting action worked out perfect for him. Nick now has to call $40 with a pot of $260. **That's 6.5 to 1 pot odds with a draw to the nut straight and three opponents.** Easy call.

THE TURN: Ace.

The board now reads K-Q-7-A.
Let's see what everyone has now…
Matt: A pair of queens and a gut-shot straight draw.
Nick: Nut straight.
Mark: Top two pair.
Fish: Bottom set.

The Pot is now $307. Mark checks. Nick checks.

I'll stop this right here. Nick has hit his draw in a big pot and then made a classic mistake. You can't go for the check raise when it is obvious to everyone at the table that the J-T just "got there". You also can't give a free card and let someone fill up or hope that your opponents bet your hand for you when such a scare card drops. There are too many players in this hand to give a free card here.

ANALYSIS: First of all, when a pot gets big, you need to take it down! Immediately! **Do not slow play when the pot gets big**…bet out and take that $300 pot and put it next to all of your other chips. Also, you will often find that **a great place to put in a big bet is on the turn**. People with draws that haven't yet hit still feel that they have a chance. When the pot gets big, some players will call almost any bet to see if they can get lucky and hit their draw. If they want to try and get lucky against you, you need to charge them a hefty price. If you check the turn with a made hand and let your opponents try and catch up for free, you are losing money no matter what hits on the river. If they make a hand that beats you, you can lose a lot of money to their river bet. If they miss their draw, they won't call a big bet so you will also lose the money that they would have called on the turn. **Never check the turn with the nuts in a large, multiplayer pot!**

Because of all the action pre-flop, Nick should conclude that there are some quality hands out there. When you are lucky enough to hit your draw, you should never be satisfied with the size of the pot. If Nick decides that at least one of his opponents has two pair or a set, he might think a bet of $100 will work. However, he must also take into account the number of opponents. If Mark calls $100 (and he probably will with top two pair), the pot has now grown to $500 and Fish is now getting 5-1 odds to call with his set. I can assure you that Fish will try to pair the board and win some more money on the river. **He must realize the probability that at least one Ace or King is gone, so he has less outs to pair the board**. Even if he figured himself for 8.5 outs the implied odds are very good. However, many players don't take all of this into account when they are making their decisions. They are just seeing a normal, logical increase in bet size in comparison to the pot. They expect to have to put more money on each street. One of the benefits of playing NLH is that you can shock your opponent with a big bet at any time. The player called $15 or $20 per flop and $30 to $40 on the flop and then all of a sudden they are looking at a $200 bet on the turn when they are still just on a draw. **Top players will never stop calculating the pot odds or probability of making a winning hand,** but many other players that you come across at the table will just stare at that big bet, shake their head and fold.

WHAT WHOULD HERO HAVE DONE?

HERO would make a big bet here…about $200. With the pot now at $300, it is in HERO'S best interest to take down the pot right now. The great part, of course, is if one of more of his opponents decides to call and the river brings a blank, HERO can make another big bet on the river and when he scoops the huge pot, he will have maximized his win with the nuts.

SUMMARY

You should always know exactly how much is in the pot.

Protect your big pairs pre-flop by making strong bets. Avoid multi-way pots.

Always understand the pot odds your bet is offering your opponent.

It is generally a mistake to make bets for less than 50% of the pot.

Do not try to set a trap in a multi-way pot.

Always bet your big hands.

Be aware of your table image. You want to be feared! Your opponents need to know that they will not be allowed to draw against you.

CHAPTER TWO
SHOWING WEAKNESS

No limit is set up to take advantage of weak players. Many top players are just looking for an opportunity to put an opponent to the test if and when they show weakness. That is one of the reasons position is so important in this game. But having position on your opponents does not solve all of your problems. This chapter will show you some of the mistakes that you must avoid if you want to be a more consistent winner at NLH.

The game in all these examples will be the same:
No Limit Tournament with 200 entrants. All players involved in hand have 3000 chips.

Mistake #4: GIVING CREDIT TOO EASILY

THE HANDS: **Fish has J-J**. Brian has 8-8. Blinds are at 50/100.

PRE FLOP: Fish makes it $300 to go pre-flop. Brian called $300 on the button. Both blinds fold.

THE FLOP: A-3-7 rainbow.

The pot contains $750. Fish checks. Brian bets $500. Fish folds.

ANALYSIS: This is a perfect example of being scared of the Ace. Fish got a perfect situation, going heads up with his pair of Jacks instead of having to try to get them to stand up in a multi-way pot. He was hoping for a perfect flop of all under-cards. This way he could bet with confidence. The one card he was hoping wouldn't make an appearance? The Ace of course.

In his mind, he had already given Brian credit for calling the pre-flop raise with a decent ace. When the ace came, he was upset and decided just to check. He hopes that if Brian doesn't have the Ace, he would play nice and check and then they could see the turn. When Brian puts in a decent sized bet, Fish decides that he must have the Ace.

Of course you can see the flaw in his thinking. This isn't a bad flop at all for a pair of Jacks. There isn't any scary draws out there and only one over-card. Fish clearly should have led out at this pot and not shown weakness. **When Fish shows weakness, Brian is going to bet at this flop with any two cards.** He is going to represent the Ace and try to take this pot down…which is what you have do in tournaments. **You cannot wait to have made hands to take down pots if you want to go far in a tournament. If you are heads up and your opponent shows weakness, you must make an attempt to take down the pot and collect some chips.**

WHAT WOULD HERO HAVE DONE?

HERO would have made a normal continuation bet with confidence. A $450-$500 bet sounds about right. **There is plenty of opportunity to outguess yourself when you are out**

of position, but the easiest way to overcome this is by not showing weakness and making a strong lead at the pot. More than likely Brian will fold his pair of eights since it appears he is beat and there are only two cards in the deck that would likely improve his hand. .

Mistake #5: CHECKING AND FOLDING TO SCARE CARD ON RIVER

THE HANDS: Hal has A-K. **Fish has K-Ts of hearts**. Ted has 6-7. The blinds are at 25/50.

PRE-FLOP ACTION: Hal opens the pot for $150. Fish calls one off the button. Ted calls on the button. The blinds both fold.

THE FLOP: 4-5-T with 2 clubs.

Hal checks. Fish leads out with a good sized bet of $400 into a $525 pot. Ted calls with position and an open ended straight draw. Hal folds.

THE TURN: Queen of hearts.

Fish now bets $300 into a pot that his now $1325. Ted calls.

THE RIVER: Jack of clubs.

Fish checks. Ted bets $1500 into a pot of $1925. Fish folds.

ANALYSIS: After a nice bet on the flop, Fish showed weakness on both the turn and river. He was essentially begging for this pot to be taken away from him when the third club came on the river.

First of all, **you should never bet less on the turn than you did on the flop**. This is screaming to everyone at the table that you like your hand less now than when you bet the flop and that means you are worrying about the strength of your hand. **In NLH, if a tough opponent thinks you doubt the strength of your hand, they will put you to the test every time.** To further the point, betting the same amount on the turn as you did the flop is also weak.

Besides that, what kind of hand could Ted have called the flop with? If he had an over-pair, wouldn't he have likely raised pre-flop or at least on the flop? If he had a set or 54 for two pair he would have also likely raised to cut off the draws...remember that on the flop he still had to worry about Hal hanging around and Hal would have had good odds to call if he was on a flush draw. So we have to put Ted on a draw or a medium pair.

When Ted senses weakness, he probably sees an opportunity to give himself more outs. What that means is that Ted might decide right now that if the club flush comes on the river and Fish checks it to him, he is going to put Fish to the test with a big bet. **It is always important to be thinking one and two steps ahead of the play of the game so your bets appear natural and it is harder to pick off your bluffs.** Ted really can't be sure that Fish isn't betting a flush draw himself (*his smaller bet on the turn actually looks like it could be a weak semi-bluff*) but Ted can be sure that if Fish is betting his flush draw, and it hits on the river, Fish will bet out instead of checking. So now Ted might feel that he can win with any 3, any 8 or any club if Fish checks the club.

When the club falls on the river, Fish seals his fate by checking. Now Ted fires out $1500, an amount that is five times the size of the turn bet. Fish can only shake his head and curse his bad luck. He is now looking at a board with two over-cards and three clubs. He might think that there is a chance his tens are good, but he would be basically betting his entire tournament on it. He folds and hopes for a better opportunity.

WHAT WOULD HERO HAVE DONE?

When the third club fell on the river, Fish could not have been pleased. However, this is no time to show weakness. **You must still play to win the pot and you must remember your table image...that doesn't mean that you let your ego get in the way of making good decisions, but it does mean that you don't want to be viewed as a passive opponent who will give up whenever a scare card comes.** The pot size is $1925. Both players have $2150. The largest bet that Fish has made so far was $400 and he has yet to be raised by his opponent (*however if HERO was in the hand, he would have made a much larger bet on the turn that would have been very hard for Ted to call).* A bet of $750 will be a good defensive bet.

Defensive bets are very important in NLH. They are bets made when you are out of position on the river when you think that you have the best hand but you really don't want to call a big bet to find out and you don't think that your opponent would raise you unless they had a better hand than you. By betting $750 at the river, Fish is telling his opponent that he still likes his hand. Ted might start thinking that Fish hit a flush on the river and is just making a value bet. *It takes a very special opponent to raise in this position without a big flush and since Ted has nothing but a missed straight draw, he will probably fold meekly and Fish will rake in a good pot.* It is much harder for your opponents to make a raise-bluff when you have made a nice bet at the river.

If you check and show weakness, when they bet you are putting a lot of pressure on yourself to come up with a perfect read and that is not the way to play winning poker.

Mistake #6 – CHECKING WHEN THE BOARD PLAYS

THE HANDS: **Fish has 8-8**. Phil has 4-4. Blinds are at 25/50.

THE TURN: 5-6-7-8

Fish had made raise pre-flop to $125 and Phil called. Fish had bet $250 on flop and Phil called. Fish bet $500 on turn and Phil called. The pot is now $1825.

Fish has top set and Phil has ignorant end of the straight.

THE RIVER: 9

The board now shows a straight of 5-6-7-8-9. Fish checks. Phil goes all in. Fish folds.

ANALYSIS: This was actually a bad card in both players mind when it fell. They both had good reason to think their hand was the best going into the river, but know it really didn't matter. No matter what their opponent has, the very best they can hope for now is a chopped pot. When Fish checks, he is in essence putting up the white flag. It is true that he could be setting a trap, but unless Phil has seen Fish trap before or has an incredible read on him, he can generally take this check to mean that he is ready to chop the pot. Phil sees almost $2000 in the pot with little risk of losing and aggressively decides to put Fish to the ultimate test for all his chips. **This is a difficult call for Fish because he would be putting his entire tournament on the line in a situation where the best he could hope for is a chop pot.** He knows that he can't win the entire pot so he must be certain that Phil does not have a Ten in his hand to make the call. Even if you think that Fish should call, you can see that this is not a decision that you want to have to make and it all happened because of a weak play. You might think, "*if he did have the Ten why would he have bet so much?*" That's the beauty of the board. Since it looks like it will be a chopped pot, a player with a ten might push all-in because the large over-bet looks like it could be a steal-bluff.

WHAT WOULD HERO HAVE DONE?

I stress over and over again in this book that having position on your opponent is a key to success, but do you see how Fish could have taken advantage of betting first? Now he would have been putting the pressure on Phil to make a tough call. **Strong players consistently put their opponents to difficult decisions**. HERO would have seen the probability of the chopped pot and tried to take the hand down for himself. Sure, Phil could have a ten in his hand, but **you have to take chances in tournaments if you are going to be a champion** and this is a perfect opportunity to take a chance. HERO has been leading out at every street and has never once shown weakness. If he feels that he would only be raised if Phil has a Ten, he can make a defensive bet (*as described in mistake #5*) of about $1000. This looks like it could be a value bet and it might be difficult for Phil to call knowing that he can't hope for anything better than a chopped pot.

However, the difference here has to be if HERO would fold if he got raised....and this is where it is very important to know your opponent. If HERO has a good read on the type of player Phil is and HERO is confident that Phil would only raise with the Ten in his hand, then he can go ahead and make this defensive bet. However, if he thinks that Phil might raise without the Ten (*if Phil is a tricky, aggressive player*) and HERO knows that he will probably call a raise and doesn't want to be left with that decision, he could go all in now and put all of the pressure on Phil to make the correct call. **Again, this might seem like a risky play because he can't win a showdown, the players that win tournaments are the players that take chances and seize every opportunity to take down pots.**

SUMMARY

You should try to avoid getting involved in pots from early position.

If you are out of position with a good hand, take the lead in the hand by betting out at the pot. If you check, expect a good opponent to bet into you and put you to a decision.

Good, aggressive players are always looking for an opportunity to put their opponents to a difficult decision

Play the entire hand in your mind before the cards fall. Look to bet. Unless you are setting a trap and you are sure that you will call any bet, avoid having to make difficult, border line decisions by making defensive bets with medium strength hands.

Look for scare cards that you can bet if your opponents check or that you can lead out with out of position.

In tournaments, champions go after pots in an aggressive, calculated manner. To get chips, you must take your share of risks. Look for good opportunities to take advantage of players that show weakness.

CHAPTER THREE
BAD BLUFFS

If you want to have consistent success at NLH, you need to know how to bluff. The bluff is a weapon in every great player's arsenal and it is something that you need to be able to do without fear of being caught. There is nothing more satisfying to the poker player's ego than winning a nice sized pot with a worse hand than his/her opponent. That being said, you first must learn what not to do. Many mistakes are made by players attempting to bluff. Here are three of the most common:

The game in all of these examples will be the same:
9 handed cash game with $5/$10 blinds. Average stack size is $800.

Mistake #7: POOR RISK/REWARD RATIO

THE HANDS: **Fish has 8-9 of diamonds**. Doug has T-T.

PRE-FLOP ACTION: Fish raises to $30. Doug calls and both blinds fold.

THE FLOP: A-3-7 with 2 diamonds.

On the flop Fish checks and Doug checks.

THE TURN: 3 of hearts.

The board now reads A-3-7-3.

Fish bets $50 with his diamond draw. Doug calls. The Pot is now $167.

THE RIVER: 10 of spades.

Fish has missed his flush draw. Doug has made a full house of Tens over Threes.

Fish bets $400 into the pot. Doug calls and takes down a very nice pot!

ANALYSIS: The hand seemed very common until the river. First there was a normal pre-flop raise. Then Fish elected to check his diamond flush instead of betting it...not aggressive but nothing unordinary. He might have been looking to check raise Doug on the flop.

When Doug checks on the flop as well, Fish assumes the Doug probably doesn't have much of a hand. With two diamonds on the flop, Doug would probably have bet a set or big ace because he can't let the draw get there cheaply.

When the turn brings a harmless 3, Fish tries to lead out at the pot and take it down. His bet might work if Doug had nothing, but with a pair of Tens, Doug probably feels he has the best hand so he calls the small bet. Since he has position and a very mediocre hand, there is no need for him to raise the small bet by Fish.

The river Ten of spades. Fish misses his flush draw. He doesn't think that Doug has the Ace or a Three so he attempts to bluff the river and take down the pot with nothing. There is nothing wrong with this type of thinking. The pot now contains $167. Fish now bets $400 to win a pot that only contains $167. By betting this much, he needs to win this hand over 70% of the time to show a profit. This is a terrible risk/reward ratio.

Not only is he risking way too much to win this pot, his bets just don't make any sense! What hand would Fish logically make this bet with? None that I can think of; except a bluff that is! **When you attempt a bluff, you are trying to tell your opponent that you have a certain hand.** He must be trying to attempt to represent a three or a full house, but does this look like the kind of bet Fish would make with a three or a full house? This does not look like the kind of bet you can expect a worse hand to call you with. If he had a very strong hand, wouldn't he have made a smaller bet to get some value out of his hand? And since Doug never shows any strength in the hand, why would Fish think Doug would have the kind of hand that could call a $400 bet if Fish had a good hand and he wanted to get paid? **This is a very confusing bet and when your opponents are confused, they are more likely to call than fold. A bluff works if it is believable. If you want to represent a hand, all of your actions throughout the hand need to tell your opponents that it is likely you have that hand**. Even if Doug did not make a full house on the river, he might call this river bet with a pair of tens because the bet does not add up and it really looks like Fish knows he could not win with a showdown, only with a bluff.

And why didn't Doug raise with his full house? First of all, this bet has to confuse the heck out of him. What in the world is Fish doing? Doug can lose to only two hands: A-A or 3-3. And it sure doesn't look like Fish has either of those hands or he wouldn't have made such a big bet...however, if Doug was to re-raise all in, what worse hand would Fish call him with? Doug and everyone else must strongly suspect that Fish is running a bluff, and if that is the case, why raise? Fish won't call if he is bluffing, but he would call with A-A or 3-3. I know it doesn't seem like he has one of those hands, but I have seen it before. It might be a cautious play, but there are many times when you have a good hand and your opponent has either nothing or a monster. Sometimes just calling on the river with a very strong hand is the best way to play.

WHAT WOULD HERO HAVE DONE?

As you can see from Doug's hand, no bluff on the river is going to work. Doug has just hit one of his two outs to make a full house and he will surely call any amount. That being said, given the way the hand was played, from HERO's perspective it would seem like a bluff might work. The pot was $167 and Doug had checked a flush draw on the flop and only called the small turn bet. HERO would bet $125-$150 at the river. This would look like a believable bet with a Three, big Ace or full house. If Doug had not hit his ten on the river, it would be very hard for him to call this bet because the entire play is believable.

Mistake #8: POOR TABLE IMAGE

THE HANDS: Fish has K-Qs. Will has T-8s.

PRE-FLOP ACTION: Fish raised to $40 pre-flop. Will called on the button. Both blinds fold.

FLOP: J-T-4.

Fish leads out for $50 with an open-ended straight draw and two over cards. Will calls.

TURN: 5.

Fish bets $100 and Will calls.

THE RIVER: 4.

Fish misses his straight draw and bets $150 with King high. Will calls with second pair and wins the pot.

ANALYSIS: You can look at the above example and not see anything wrong with Fish's actions. He decided to take an aggressive approach on this hand when he flopped the straight draw. He continued betting into Will on every street. He increased the size of his bet every step of the way. It sure looked like the actions of a player with a strong hand.

However, what you do not know is that *Fish has been bluffing all night long*! Not only has he been bluffing, but he has been *caught* bluffing continuously. **Fish has an incredibly loose and reckless table image. He has not yet shown down a solid hand. Everyone at the table knows that Fish will bet with nothing because they have seen it so many times.** Fish, however, has not realized yet. Sure, he has been unlucky to miss his draws all night long *(it happens to all of us from time to time)* but he has continued to bet the river when his draw does not get there and his bets are getting no respect.

Every time you play poker your situations change. You must constantly be aware of the conditions that you are playing under. What is the mood of the table? How are the players reacting to each other? What is your table image? Have any of these variables changed since you sat down? Maybe you are playing with a regular group and they normally view you as a tight, straightforward player but tonight you showed a bluff early and now your table image has changed. This happens all the time and it is much more important to be aware of all of these factors than many players realize.

When you have been caught bluffing a few times, you need to be able to change gears. You wanted to play aggressive poker and bluff more often tonight, but now all of that has changed. Now you need to stop bluffing until you can show down a few quality hands and take down a few pots. Maybe you need to tighten up for the next hour and let everyone at the table think that you have decided to go back to your normal, solid game before changing gears once again and attempting another bluff. **Remember, a bluff only works when you can get your opponents to believe you, and some nights they just won't believe anything that you are selling.** This might stop some of your bluff attempts, but on a positive note, it will help you get paid more when you have a real hand. **Now you need to look to make more value bets because you will probably get called by worse hands.**

WHAT WOULD HERO HAVE DONE?

Being aware of his reckless, bluffing table image, HERO would have taken a different approach. Knowing that his opponent would call a bet with any piece of that board, HERO might have opted to check the flop with this reasoning: If Will did hit that board, he might check hoping to induce HERO to bluff at the turn. HERO would try to use this table image to his advantage and see the turn for free. If HERO was able to make his straight on the turn, he would lead into Will knowing that Will would call HERO down with any hand. However, if HERO bet at the flop or turn and was called, he would not bet at the river. There is too good of a chance that he would be called knowing his current table image. **When you are known to bluff, many players will try to trap you and induce you to bluff into them at the river**. You can use this to your advantage by giving yourself free cards on earlier streets.

Mistake #9: BLUFFING INTO TOO MANY PLAYERS

THE HANDS: **Fish has T-9**. Tom has K-Q. Kurt has A-Js. Paul has 4-4. Kim has K-T.

PRE-FLOP ACTION: Fish and Tom limp. Kurt raises to $30. Paul calls. Kim calls from one of the blinds. Fish and Tom call when it comes back to them.

THE FLOP: 6-7-2

Everyone checks the flop.

THE TURN: 6

Everyone checks the turn.

THE RIVER: J.

Kim checks. Fish bets $80. Kurt calls. Everyone else folds. Kurt wins with two pair (JJ,66).

ANALYSIS: When the action gets checked around twice, it is safe to assume that no one has anything. However, the river brings a Jack and if any of Fish's four opponents has a Jack in their hand, Fish will probably get called. The pot has $155. By betting $80, it does appear that Fish could be betting for value here, but he will still get called by a Jack since the pot odds are so good for his opponent. If the action got folded around to Paul with his pocket fours, he might want to be the sheriff getting almost 3-1 pot odds on what could be a bluff. Fish is just betting into too many opponents to make this bluff successful enough times to be profitable.

Outside of the fact that there are too many opponents, **is there a different card that could have fallen on the river that might have presented a better bluffing opportunity?**

When Fish bets at this river he is obviously representing that he has a Jack in his hand. That will work unless someone has a Jack in there hand and there is no way of knowing either way whether anyone has a Jack.

What if another seven fell on the river? It would be a much better card to bluff at because only a few hands can call this bet. You can be pretty sure that no one has a seven or an over-pair or else they would have bet on the flop or turn. Anyone with a pair of deuces just got counterfeited. The only hands that you worry about is someone holding a 6 or if someone has an Ace and suspects that you might have the same hand or are just on a stone cold bluff. Hopefully, you can see that although the seven is the best card that could drop if you want to bluff, with so many opponents it is still very risky to think that your bluff will work because there are so many different hands that they could hold.

WHAT WOULD HERO HAVE DONE?

A bluff works best when you are heads up. Two opponents can be bluffed enough times for it to be profitable. With more than two opponents, your chances for success continue to decrease. If HERO had decided to bluff at this pot, he would have led at the turn for $75. If he got called by only one opponent, he would have to decide if that opponent had a 6. If HERO felt that his opponent did not have a 6 in his hand, he would have led $150 at the river. HERO would not bet into more than one person in this situation because it would have been too likely that one of them had a 6 and would not fold the hand.

Mistake #10 - NEVER BLUFFING

This would be the biggest mistake of them all. **If you want to play NLH and you want to win consistently, then you must be able to bluff successfully**. There are situations where it is correct to bluff with more or less frequency, but **there are no occasions where it is correct to never bluff.** Many amateur players are afraid of being caught bluffing, but they shouldn't for many reasons.

First of all, when you do get a "real hand" after you have been caught bluffing, you will have a much better chance of winning more money. A common expression is "*you have to give action to get action*" because if the table knows you will bluff from time to time, someone might call your big bet with a mediocre hand hoping to pick off your bluff. **Never bluffing leads to rarely getting your big bets "paid off".**

Also, there will be some nights when you simply do not catch any cards. Do you just want to give in to the "luck" factor of poker? You don't have to when playing NLH. **You just need to make sure you play position poker and try to isolate those players that you feel are capable of laying down a good hand**. Look for good bluff situations, but be patient. Before the cards are dealt, you can't simply say "I am going to bluff this hand no matter what happens" because you have no information. The reason professionals can win consistently at poker is because they make good decisions based on information they get at the table. If you decided bluff no matter what happens and then the tightest player at the table raises under the gun, you probably need to rethink bluffing on this hand because that player probably has a real hand!

Wait for the right situation to happen and then go for it.

SUMMARY

Ask yourself what hand you are trying to represent and then decide if your bet makes sense for that hand. You do not want to confuse your opponent when you bluff.

Make sure the size of your bet gives you a good risk/reward ratio.

You will have a greater chance of a successful bluff when you are only up against one opponent.

Always understand your table image. Have you been caught bluffing recently? Do your opponents seem to always think you are bluffing?

Don't get upset when you get caught bluffing. Now you have a better chance of getting paid off when you get a strong hand. If you have been caught bluffing more than once, make sure you try betting more than you normally do when you have a 'real hand' because your opponents might still think you are bluffing and decide to call you down with a mediocre hand.

Certain cards are better for you to bluff at. Try to always determine which cards would be good bluff cards and play them accordingly.

A tip for tournaments - If you never get caught bluffing or stealing blinds, then you are doing something wrong.

SECTION TWO
MENTAL MISTAKES

All players know to fold a deuce – seven under the gun and raise with pocket aces. Many players can come to agreement on common game play decisions regarding calling, folding and raising. In many situations, if players are able to count their probable outs and know the pots odds, they can mathematically come the up the correct decision.

What separates the successful winning professional from his often losing amateur opponents is the ability to be mentally focused on the game. The professional is focused on his opponents and the game environment. He is gathering information on every hand and using that information to make better decisions than everyone else at the table. The pro avoids letting his mind wander to other issues and events away from the game. The mental mistakes detailed in this section must be avoided by any player looking to become a consistent winning player.

CHAPTER FOUR

PAY ATTENTION

The reason a top professional can win consistently at poker is because of his decision making skill. He is paying attention to all of his opponents during each hand that is being played, whether or not he is in the hand himself. During every hand, your opponents are giving the skilled observer information on how they play poker. Their actions are giving the professional information which he will use to make his decisions.

Even when they are both intently watching their opponents, the thing that separates a successful professional from a struggling amateur is what they are watching for.

The amateur might notice that the player in seat one is very aggressive, always raising or re-raising pots. He wants to avoid playing a pot with this player.

The pro would also notice that this opponent is aggressive but he would also notice that the player will announce his raise to the table when he has a good hand, but when he is bluffing he will not say a word as he pushes his chips into the pot with two hands. They both agree that he is raising a lot but the pro already has an understanding of when he needs to call that player and when he needs to get out of his way.

The key to playing winning poker is making good decisions, and the key to making good decisions is paying attention. This chapter is going to show you what you need to be looking for so that you will be paying attention to the right things.

Mistake #11: NOT KNOWING YOUR OPPONENT

Weak opponents might as well be playing with their cards face up. They make the same type of bets with the same hands all the time. They are telling you what they hold by the way they are betting. And they will do so in a consistent manner so that you will know how to attack these players when you play them in a pot. You need to identify their playing style as quickly as possible to help you make better decisions when you are playing against them.

Some questions to be asking yourself when you are watching your opponents:

What hands will my opponent re-raise with pre-flop?

It is very important to note how many different hands your opponent will re-raise with pre-flop. Some players telegraph the strength of their hand by only re-raising with aces or kings. Notice what hands the player that re-raised is showing down. If you have a pair of queens pre-flop and you get re-raised by the button, you need to know whether that player will re-raise with anything less than kings.

Does my opponent look to trap or bet out?

Many top professionals advise betting out whenever flopping a big hand. Still, many players will check their hands on the flop when they flop two pair or better. They instinctively look to trap you. Especially if you make good pot size bets they will hope that you bet their hand for them.

Here are some patterns to look for from your opponent when they flop big hands:

- Check and call the flop, lead out at the turn.
- Check and call the flop, check and call the turn, lead out at the river.
- If they check raise you need to look for what street they normally look to do so.

However, more important would be to try to identify those players that lead out at their big hands. I have seen players lead out even when they have flopped quads.

The key again is to look for players who seem to do one or the other every time.

Does he ever check raise?

Some players fall in love with this move and will use it all of the time while other players never use it. It is important to note if your opponents use this move because you will then find opportunities to give yourself a free card. Also, if you like to bet your draws aggressively, you will often find yourself in trouble against a check raise.

Here is an example:

You hold JT of diamonds. The board is AK26 with two diamonds. The pot size is $50. Your opponent checks the turn and you bet $50 with your flush draw and gut-shot straight draw. Your opponent check raises you all-in for $300 more.

This happens all of the time and now you would be making a mistake to call this bet with only a draw (the pot is now $450 and it will cost you $300 to call and see the river). You could have seen the river for free if you realized your opponent likes to check raise.

Does my opponent bet his draws?
Would he bet all-in with just a draw?
Will he call an all-in bet with just a draw?

There is a big difference in the above questions. Some opponents play their draws very aggressively and love to semi-bluff their draws with big bets. You will find some opponents make bigger bets when they are drawing than when they actually have a made hand. Betting all-in with a draw is a lot different than calling and all-in bet with a draw. If the pot size if $100 and you go all in for $300 with a diamond draw on the board, a good player will realize that he is not getting good enough odds to call this over-bet and will lay down the draw. Other weaker players might just want to gamble and call the all-in bet because they like playing big pots. Knowing your opponents will help you when playing pots with draws on the board.

Will my opponent bluff?
When my opponent bluffs how much does he bet?
When my opponent bluffs, does he bet on every street?

Some players will over-bet bluff (*the pot is $50 and they bet $150*) and some will under-bet bluff (*the pot is $100 and they bet $20*). If your opponent bets his draws, then he probably will bluff on every street (on the flop and turn he is semi-bluffing and when his draw misses the river, he is on a cold-stone bluff).

Many players that will lead out for a bluff on the flop, check the turn if they get called on the flop, and if their opponent checks on the turn, they will again bluff-lead out on the river. This is why it is so important to watch all of the action when you are not in a hand. There is so much about the way your opponents play that you need to be aware…and you can find out everything if you just watch them. The more you know about how your opponent bluffs, the easier it will be for you to play your mediocre holdings.

Is my opponent capable of laying down good hands (*which means they are bluffable*)? Will my opponent call with any piece of the board because they hate being bluffed?

Will this player make a continuation bet at the flop but then check the turn if he has nothing?

A continuation bet is made when the pre flop raiser misses the flop but continues his aggressive approach to the hand by betting the flop. This move is made by most NLH cash game players. The pattern that you are looking to uncover is what he does next. When your opponent is called on the flop, will he then shut down and check and flop on the turn? Will your opponent only stop betting into you if he is raised? When you find yourself playing against a predictable opponent, you can see how any two cards can win.

You need to know what hands your opponent will play and how they will play them on every betting street. You then need to decide on a game plan for each opponent.

Poor players give off tells. By their actions during the course of a hand, they are "telling" you what they think of their hand. The skill of reading players is something that all successful players posses, but it definitely comes easier for some players than others. It is a skill that can be learned with practice.

One of the easiest tell to pick up on weak players is in their betting pattern. When it is their turn to bet, they will

generally repeat certain actions based on if they are bluffing or if they hold a real hand. You should always be asking yourself questions about your opponents as you watch them in action.

Here is an example of questions you can be asking yourself as you watch them bet...

Do they announce their bet or just put the chips in the pot?

How do they count their chips?

Is there anything significant to how they normally put their chips in the pot?

How does your opponent stack his chips?

Does he place them down gently or does he forcefully slam them down?

Why does all this matter? Because players tend to do the same pattern betting good hands and betting poor hands. Wouldn't it be easier to play if you knew exactly what your opponent had? By watching how he bets and then remembering what hand he shows at showdown, you should have a better idea if any type of pattern is being established.

Recognize what they normally do and then see what happens. If the player turns over a strong hand at showdown, which of the two actions did they do? If they haven't been saying a word, just pushing the chips in the pot, and they have been showing good, strong hands...but now they announce their bet loud and proud, pay very close attention to their hand if it is shown. Maybe they are now running a bluff. This is a common mistake for weak players...and they don't even know they are doing it. They have a normal way of putting their chips in the pot and a different way of putting them in the pot when they are bluffing.

Here are a couple of examples of what I mean:

I remember playing against one opponent who, when it was his turn to bet, would usually grab a big handful of chips, announce his bet ("$30 to go"), and then count out his chips in the middle of the betting ring (for those of you who have not played in live casinos, many tables have a visible ring in the middle considered the betting area). However, when he had a very good hand he would take much longer and count his chips out in front of him, behind the betting area, then when he felt he had the right amount for bet, he would just push his chips into the middle without saying a word. That might not seem like a big difference but for those who knew the tell, it told us what how strong he felt his hand was. This is a very important element to winning at NLH.

I remember playing against a very good friend who would bet with bigger chips if he was bluffing. If he wanted to bet $75, he would normally bet fifteen $5 chips. However, when he was bluffing and trying to "buy" the pot, he would bet three $25 chips.

You can take advantage of this information best when you play in a regular home game with the same friends/opponents. If you really pay attention to their actions, the next time you go against them you will be surprised how easy you can make the proper decision.

This doesn't mean that you shouldn't be paying as much attention to the players at the local casino because you never know when you will see these players again and how much money will be on the line when you are in a hand against them and you are facing a tough decision. The most successful professionals have a tremendous memory and it helps them to make winning decisions.

Mistake #12: NOT NOTICING CHANGES TO ENVIRONMENT

A sold poker player understands that every table is different. Each table is filled with different players, with different theories on how to play each hand. Some tables are tight and some are loose. Some are passive and some aggressive. However, you can never forget that everyone at the table is human, and therefore subject to change and of course, tilt. A successful professional understands that every table is a forever changing environment.

Especially after a big pot has been played, you need to ask yourself the following questions if you want to keep up on the changes:

Has my table image changed at all?

Did you just get caught bluffing?
Maybe you shouldn't attempt another bluff for awhile. You should probably bet a little more than you usually do with your medium to strong holdings because there is now a greater chance that you will be called by weaker hands. Did you give off any tells when you were bluffing? Did you bet in a certain manner? Where were you looking? What, if anything, were you saying? Now you have to try to repeat all of your actions that you did when you were bluffing the next time you are betting for value so that the players will be unable to pick up any tells.

Did you just call a large bet with a weak holding because you suspected an opponent might be bluffing?
When you make this call, it's not really going to matter if your opponent was really bluffing or if he had a hand as long as your hand is shown. Most of your opponents are going to understand what you were doing.
Are players going to stop attempting bluffs into you now? Are

players going to start betting for value more against you because they don't think you can throw away your hand? Did your opponent give off any tell (bet in a certain way, look a certain way) when he was bluffing (or when you thought that he was bluffing but he wasn't)? Remember what you saw for future reference.

Did you just win a hand in which you were trapping? Check raise your opponent?
Now you might be able to get more free cards out of position. Your opponents won't want to bet their semi-strong holdings because they fear your check does not mean weakness.

Did you suck-out on your opponent? Call a big bet with only a draw? Make a huge bet with only a draw?
Anytime you win a hand (especially a big pot) your opponents will start to get information about the way you play and you will start creating a certain table image. Your image can change after one hand though, and you must be aware of it because your opponents will play differently against you according to your image. As you can see, winning NLH is about so many other things than the cards themselves.

Not only should you be asking all of these questions about yourself, but you should also ask them about your opponents when you are not involved in the hand.

What are your opponents' table images?

Has your impression of their image changed at all recently?

Did someone lose a big pot and now on tilt, playing far worse than they normally do because they have let emotion cloud their judgment?

How should this affect the way you play against them?

Other changes in environment that affect play:

A player has left the game and a seat is open. A new player has entered the game. All it takes is one loose, reckless player to change the entire table. If that player is loose and reckless, where is he/she sitting? Do they have position on you? Can you change seats so that you have position on all of the aggressive players? A simple rule of thumb: tight and passive players to your left, loose and aggressive players to your right. Whenever there is an open seat, try to move so that you have the best players to the table on your right.

Is there a new "big stack"?
This is more important in tournament play, but I know many cash game players that play different (more aggressive) when they are winning and have a lot of chips in front of them. Many times in tournament play, if a big hand has just ended and a new player has emerged as the chip leader or has gone from a medium sized stack to a large stack, the entire table will change. If this player is playing his big stack properly, he will start picking on the smaller stacks and raising with more hands than he was previously playing.

A player is about to leave soon.
They might have been talking about it with a friend or someone at the table. You know they are going to leave after a few more hands. What does this mean? If they are way ahead, they might play a hand more timid and passive because they don't want to loose all of their winnings right before they go home. Or if they are behind they might want to gamble more and take greater chances with a hope of getting even. Either way they will probably enter the pot with at least once with a hand that they wouldn't otherwise play because they want to see one more flop before they go.

CHAPTER FIVE
EVERYTHING BUT THE CARDS

Poker is mental war-fare and No Limit poker is so emotional that you must mentally prepare yourself for battle if you want to have consistent success. If you are tired, sick, in a bad mood or just not able to focus mentally because other factors in your life, you are playing with a big disadvantage. You can't control the cards that are dealt to you, but you can control your actions at the table.

Mistake # 13: GIVING LESSONS AT THE TABLE

If you frequent a local card room, then you either know or have witnessed the player at your table who thinks that he knows everything about winning poker and wants to show off. He is constantly telling other players at the table what they are doing wrong and what they should be doing in certain situations. Let's call this player PHIL. This player may or may not know correct poker strategy, but either way he is ruining the game!

First of all, if you have bad players playing against you, you should be celebrating. Sharks don't eat other sharks! They eat smaller, weaker fish. **You want to be playing against poor**

players; that is how you make money and why poker is a beatable game. Some players have a distinct advantage over other players and that is because poker is game of skill.

While PHIL is upset that he is going up against bad amateur players that may get lucky and suck-out against him, you have to understand that when you are playing winning poker, the percentages are in your favor. If you are a winning player going against bad players, **you will get sucked out on more than anyone at the table because you will be playing better hands than your opponents and they will be calling bets from you with hands that need help**. And you need to realize that your big hands will not hold up all of the time. When you have pocket aces and your opponent has pocket sevens, you will win over 80% of the time...but that also means that you will lose almost 20% of the time. You need to remember that when you lose. **Unless you have the nuts, some of the time you are going to lose even when your opponent only has a few cards in the deck that can help him. And because you will seldom put your money in the middle drawing so thin, you will seldom suck out on bad players.**

Does that mean that you don't want your opponent to call with pocket sevens when you have pocket aces? No. You should always want to be called when you are that big of a favorite. That's how you will win money. And if you do lose, that same opponent will keep making bad calls and give you plenty of chances to make that money back.

A bad player might get lucky once or twice, but over the course of time (usually in that same session) the bad player will give those chips right back to everyone at the table. **And if they are having a good, fun time at the table, the losing player will probably dig into their pockets for more money that they will also eventually lose.**

DO YOU REALLY WANT TO HELP THIS PLAYER

OUT? DO YOU REALLY WANT THIS PLAYER TO STOP CALLING BIG RAISES PRE-FLOP WITH 4-8 OFFSUIT? No. You want him to put his money in play against you when you have a substantial advantage in the hand. Let him try to catch up. **Let him keep playing this way because you will have a great chance of winning your money back and then some.**

Not only that. Usually a player like PHIL does not stop at giving lessons. He usually goes out of his way to make his opponent feel bad and embarrassed. He is looking to try to impress other players at the table with his knowledge, but he also wants the bad player to know how bad he is. Is this good for the game? No. Many times the bad player will leave (*sometimes with many chips that he was lucky to win and would have surely "given back" through bad play over the rest of the session*). If this player leaves, that money is gone too. If the player stays, he might now stop playing those crazy hands and start trying to only play the best hands so that he is not embarrassed any more. Is this what you want? Of course not.

A general rule of thumb is to be as nice as possible to the worst players in the game. You want them to enjoy themselves and have a good time. You want them to want to stick around and put that money back in play. You don't want to make them feel bad or embarrassed. And you want them to come back again in the future. You want their money so you want them to feel loose and have a good time. And after they lose, you want them to be having such a good time that they head off to the ATM to reload. These players probably didn't expect to win when they came to the table…they just wanted to have a good time playing some cards. Don't disappoint them.

Mistake #14: TILTING

We all go on tilt. The key is not to ever go on tilt, but instead to try to snap out of it as quickly as possible and to keep your degree of TILT to a minimum. Some players go on tilt when they lose a big pot or when they get rivered with a bad beat. Whatever the reason, when you are tilting, you are playing less than your best poker. You are thinking about so many things that you should not be thinking about and you start missing out on valuable information.

How can I get off tilt quickly? This is something that you need to ask yourself before you sit down. Every player is different and because tilting is emotional, you are the only one that knows how you can get off tilt.

Before you sit down at the table, before you take a bad beat or lose a huge pot, you need to take a few moments to get into the right frame of mind. Professional athletes like to visualize themselves having success before going on the field. They see themselves hit a home run or score a touchdown in their mind's eye and repeat that success in live play. As a poker player, you can do the same thing. **To win at NLH, you need to feel aggressive.** And you need to ask yourself how you can avoid tilt.

Some players have pictures of their family with them at all times. They look at the pictures of their children whenever they get upset and try to calm themselves down and remember that this is just a game. I know a few players that listen to music and when they take an especially tough beat, have a special song that they listen to. Like I said, everyone is different.

My best advice is to put it into perspective. Professional players view all of their visits to play poker as just one big session. It doesn't stop when they leave for the night and it doesn't start when they sit down and buy some chips. It is ongoing and never stops. Some times they take a bad beat and some times they deliver a bad beat. They keep meticulous records of hours played and how much is won or lost. If the pro buys into a NLH game for $500 and an hour later they lose their entire buy in, it doesn't matter if they choose to buy back for $500 that night or the next morning...**their next hour of play is going to be their next hour of play, regardless of what day or place it occurs**. The game is always going to be there for them. The rules aren't going to change. Nothing is going to change...except maybe their mood.

As long as they don't get too emotional over losing their initial $500 buy in, they will be able to play as well that night as any other night. If the game is unusually tough or they just don't feel right, by all means they should leave and play another day. But if they feel good and the games seems beatable, than they should stay as long as they have kept their emotions in check and avoided tilt.

That being said, many players give themselves a stop/loss limit because they understand that once they lose a certain amount of money, they will definitely be tilting (even though they might not notice it at the time). I know many players that will walk away from the table once they lose two buy-ins because they know that they will not be playing their best poker. This might be a good idea if you have a history of big losing sessions or if you know you are susceptible to tilting.

As stated earlier, **one thing about bad beats that professionals understand; the better players are always going to be taking more bad beats than poor players because they are going to be playing from ahead more often**. When the professional is beat or drawing thin, they will fold the hand. When the poor player is way behind, they will still call big bets because they don't understand what is going on and how far behind they really are. As a good player, you want that call from behind because that is how you make your money. And that is also why you will experience more bad beats. Just remember the next time that you are raking in a huge pot that you will have to take a bad beat once in a while to even things out.

Mistake #15: THINKING ABOUT THE MONEY

The best advice I can give anyone about gambling is this: **don't play with money you can't afford to lose.** You have probably heard this advice before and there is a reason…it is great advice. One of the reasons why you shouldn't play poker with money that you can't afford to lose is this: you will probably play worse with that money than you normally would because you would be playing scared.

NLH is a game where you must gamble and must take chances if you want to win. When you are winning consistently, you are playing your opponents hand more than your own. If you feel your opponent has nothing, then you must be able to push your chips in the middle and make him fold…regardless of what you hold. **Putting your opponents to the test is the key to NLH and to do so you can't be concerned about putting your chips at risk. If you are thinking about the money, you are playing stakes that are too high**.

Many players feel that skill level should determine what stakes they play. These players could not be more wrong. If you are a good player you understand how to play aggressively. But if you start playing stakes that you can't afford to lose, you will make some costly mistakes. Usually you see players who are thinking about money just flat call decent sized bets instead of raising and committing more money to the pot. Then they are giving their opponents more chances to draw out on them. Or they are easily bluffed because they don't want to risk a great amount of money to a marginal hand. And they very rarely bluff…they wouldn't want to risk that much money with nothing.

Don't be this player. Don't let your ego get involved. The player that sits down at a $1/$2 NLH and wins is still a winner more than someone who sits down at a $5/$10 game and goes bust. Play within your means and work on your game at levels where you can afford to lose.

FIVE KEY STEPS TO IMPROVING YOUR GAME

1. At the end of every hand, go through each decision and see if there was something you should have done differently. **On every hand, it doesn't matter if you win or lose the hand; you need to review each betting round**. *Should you have raised instead of called? Did you raise too little or too much? Did you lose more money than you should have with that hand...would you have won more if you played it differently?* Ask yourself every question imaginable. You are not doing this so that you start to second guess yourself at the poker table…you are doing this to help improve your game. You want to start coming up with a strategy to win consistently. If you see yourself making a mistake, in a way you should be pleased. That is the first step to becoming a better player. The next step is preparing you mentally to avoid making the same mistake again.

   At the end of every session, you will again review interesting hands that came up and how you handled different situations. This time you should seek out "poker friends" to discuss the hands. The poker friends that you seek for discussion can't just be the guys you hang out with. You need to look for people with a solid game that you respect. You need to look for people that will be honest with you and might have a different view than you do. **It is good to get many different points of view on a poker question.** Even if you don't agree with their opinion, it is always interesting to hear how people think while they are involved in a hand.

2. Whether you are winning or losing, remind yourself time and time again to **play more hands in late position and less hand in early position.** When I see good solid players start losing more than they should, it

is because they are playing way too many hands in early position. This forces you to make perfect decisions all the time with very little information about your opponents' hands. This is a no way to win consistently. However, when I have students that go on winning steaks and start playing with a lot of confidence, I see them start playing too many hands out of position as well because they think that they can overcome this disadvantage and still win the hand. This type of thinking generally brings the winning steak to an end. It doesn't matter how good you are or how poor the game is...playing out of position is a big disadvantage that you should try to avoid.

3. Always do the math! **You should always be keeping a running total of the pot size and the pot odds.** To win consistently at poker, you need to make better decisions than your opponents. To make better decisions when it is your turn to act, you need to understand your pot odds and the odds that you are offering your opponents through your bet. NO LIMIT HOLD 'EM allows you to manipulate the pot odds...take advantage and you will thrive. I have seen players fold on the river to a $50 bet when the pot was many hundreds of dollars. They feel that their hand is beat but in reality **when you are getting offered huge pot odds, it is almost always incorrect to fold**. Even if you had a busted straight draw and were holding king high, no pair, if the pot and the odds were large enough you would call a river bet. First of all there is always a chance your opponent is bluffing (maybe he also had a straight draw that missed but he had the lower end and he knew that the only way he could win the pot was by making a bet on the end and hoping you had nothing). Secondly, you are paying for information. If you were heads up in position and the pot had $500 in it, you would have to call a river bet of $50 or less with almost

any hand at the very least to see what your opponent had and how they played the hand. I'm not telling you that you have to play the part of the "sheriff" and always call river bets so that you won't be bluffed (It is ok to be bluffed. If you never fold the best hand you aren't playing good poker.). I am stressing the need to take into account the size of the pot when making all decisions.

4. Follow this rule always: **Never show your hands unless you have to**. You should know by now how important information about your opponents is. Showing your hands gives your toughest opponents that much more information about how you play certain hands. Maybe they picked up a tell from you and now that you have shown your cards, they know what that tell means. You always want to keep your opponents guessing and make them pay for their information.

5. Spend less time thinking about your hand and more time concentrating on your opponents' hand. You should always be asking yourself…"**What hand could my opponent have that I can beat right now?** What hand is he betting with that I can beat?" The reason so many players don't win consistently is because they are only thinking about their hand and they never take the time to put their opponent on a hand. Or more specifically, a range of hands. It is very difficult, for even the top pros, to put their opponent on one specific hand. It is much more useful and accurate to put them on a range of hands and then weigh the percentages.

   Equally important is what your opponent thinks about the strength of your own hand. **NO LIMIT is all about putting pressure on your opponents**. You need to force them to have a hand to play against you! If you feel they have a weak hand, make a big bet that will be tough for them to call. If you feel that they are on a draw that missed, make sure you put in a big bet at the river to try and win the pot.

Here are the levels of thinking in poker:

First Level – What do you have?

Second Level - What does your opponent have?

Third Level - What does your opponent think you have?

Fourth Level - What does your opponent think you think he has?

Fifth Level - What does your opponent think you think he thinks you have?

You should always be watching your opponents when you are not in the hand. Now that you don't have to worry about making any decisions, you can just concentrate on the other players and watch them for playing patterns and tells. Not only that, but you should practice guessing what hand they have while they are playing. When the hand goes to show down, or if one of the players show at the end, see how close your guess was. When you are right or wrong, review in your mind why you thought that player was strong or weak and if you were correct in your thinking. Later on when you are involved in a hand with this opponent, it might be much easier for you to put them on a hand based on all of your observations. Practice makes perfect.

Top professional players think on all levels. You need to spend less time on level one and two and start winning more consistently today!

Printed in the United States
71891LV00002B/2

9 781598 007237